Twenty-two Cents

Muhammad Yunus and the Village Bank

by **Paula Yoo**

illustrated by **Jamel Akib**

LEE & LOW BOOKS INC. • *New York*

The author would like to thank the following people for their help and support: Jason Low; Emily Hazel; my wonderful editor, Jessica Echeverria; Steven Malk; Mark Mancall, Professor of History, Emeritus, Stanford University; Simi Singh Juneja; and Ajmal Sobhan. Special thanks to Professor Muhammad Yunus; Hans Reitz, founder and managing director of Grameen Creative Lab; and everyone at the Yunus Centre, including Executive Director Lamiya Morshed, program officers Sharmen Shahria Ferdush and Shiban Mahbub, and program associate Md. Robayt Khondoker.

Manufactured in Malaysia by Tien Wah Press, January 2018
Book design by Christy Hale
Book production by The Kids at Our House
The text is set in Octavian
The illustrations are rendered in chalk pastel

(hc) 10 9 8 7 6 5 4 3 2
(pb) 10 9 8 7 6 5 4 3 2 1
First Edition

Library of Congress Cataloging-in-Publication Data
Yoo, Paula.
   Twenty-two cents: Muhammad Yunus and the Village Bank / by Paula Yoo; illustrated by Jamel Akib. — First edition.
        pages cm
   Summary: "A biography of Nobel Peace Prize winner Muhammad Yunus, who from a young age was determined to make a difference in the world and eventually revolutionized global antipoverty efforts by developing the innovative economic concept of micro-lending. Includes an afterword and author's sources"—Provided by publisher.
   ISBN 978-1-60060-658-8 (hardcover :alk. paper) ISBN 978-1-62014-809-9 (paperback)
1. Yunus, Muhammad, 1940—Juvenile literature. 2. Grameen Bank—Juvenile literature. 3. Bankers—Bangladesh—Biography—Juvenile literature. 4. Economists—Bangladesh—Biography—Juvenile literature. 5. Microfinance—Developing countries—Juvenile literature. I. Akib, Jamel, illustrator. II. Title.
HG3290.6.A8G73864 2014
332.1092—dc23   [B]   2013041045

To Professor Muhammad Yunus and his commitment to eradicating poverty from our world so no child will go to sleep hungry —P.Y.

For Mich, P., and Bean —J.A.

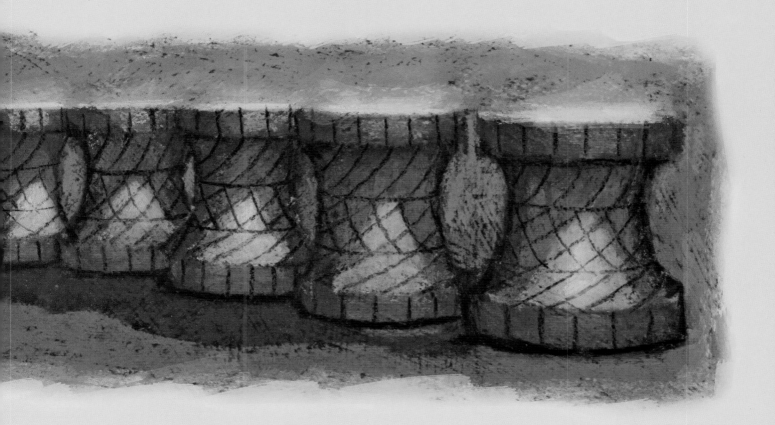

MUHAMMAD's stomach growled as he and his brothers and sisters watched their mother mix rice flour, sugar, and coconut to create the dough for sweet *pithas*. She molded the dough into oval cakes and dropped them into hot oil. Each pitha floated to the top of the pan, frying to a crispy golden brown. Then she placed the pithas on a plate to cool.

Eight-year-old Muhammad eagerly reached for a pitha. But before he could take his first bite, someone knocked on the door. Outside stood a weary woman and a little girl. The woman said they hadn't eaten in days.

Poor people often stopped by the house because Muhammad's mother was known for giving away food, money, and even clothes her children had outgrown. Muhammad knew the hungry people at the door needed the food more than he did. He placed the pitha back on the plate. His mother smiled at him as the grateful woman and child ate every crumb.

Muhammad Yunus was born on June 28, 1940, the third oldest of nine children. His Bengali family lived in a two-story house in the port city of Chittagong, then part of India. Chittagong was a bustling city. Delivery trucks rumbled past passengers riding in colorful rickshaws. Beggars wandered side by side with businessmen along the densely crowded streets. People sipped tea or ate *chanachur*, a snack made of fried lentils and chickpeas, at one of the tea stalls along the roads.

Muhammad and his siblings found many ways to have fun together. They pretended to be soldiers, chasing one another across the flat rooftop of their house. They flew kites made of bamboo and paper. And sometimes after school they were allowed to go to the movies.

Education was very important to Muhammad's parents, and they made sure their children studied hard. Although Muhammad's father, Dula Mia, was a successful jewelry maker, he had just an eighth-grade education. Muhammad's mother, Sofia Khatun, went to school only up to the fourth grade, but she was passionate about reading and reciting epic stories to her children. The parents hoped their children would finish school and one day go to college.

Dula Mia also encouraged his sons to explore the world by joining organizations such as the Boy Scouts. "Learning from the world is the greatest learning," he told them.

Muhammad liked being a Boy Scout. The boys played games, hiked in the countryside, mastered outdoor scouting skills, and worked to help the less fortunate in their community. During some scout outings, Muhammad saw the terrible conditions in the slums where poor people lived. Families were crammed into tiny shanties built of bamboo, cardboard, and rusted tin. Homeless mothers huddled with their children in alleyways overflowing with sewage. It was almost impossible for the families to find enough fresh water and clean food.

Muhammad became very active in his troop's charity activities. The Scouts hosted Earnings Weeks during which they polished boots and sold books and tea to raise money for the poor. Muhammad noticed how just a few coins could buy enough rice to feed a family for an entire week.

As he grew older, Muhammad wanted to continue helping those who were living in poverty. In 1957, at the age of seventeen, he enrolled in the Department of Economics at Dhaka University. Economics is the study of how people make and use money, goods, and services. Muhammad thought studying economics would teach him how to help the poor manage and save their money better.

After graduating from Dhaka University, Muhammad became a research assistant and lecturer. Then in 1965 he won a prestigious Fulbright scholarship to study economics in the United States. While in America, he witnessed college students holding peace rallies to show their opposition to the Vietnam War. They went on protest marches and held sit-ins, refusing to move until they were heard. Muhammad was greatly impressed by the students' belief that they could make a difference. And he remembered his father's words: he was truly learning from the world.

In 1970 Muhammad accepted a teaching job at Middle Tennessee State University. Although he was happy in the United States, Muhammad worried about the turmoil in his home country.

When British rule of India ended in 1947, Chittagong became part of what was known as East Bengal and later East Pakistan. The region was home to a large Bengali population. Due to economic, political, and cultural differences, the people of East Pakistan wanted their independence from the West Pakistani government. In March 1971 East Pakistan seceded and declared itself the independent nation of Bangladesh. Tensions continued to mount, soon leading to a war between Pakistan and the new nation of Bangladesh.

Inspired to support his people, Muhammad organized rallies on the university campus. He also went to Washington, DC, where he and other Bengalis demonstrated on the steps of Capitol Hill. They chanted for peace between Bangladesh and Pakistan. They answered questions for television and newspaper reporters to raise awareness about the situation in their homeland.

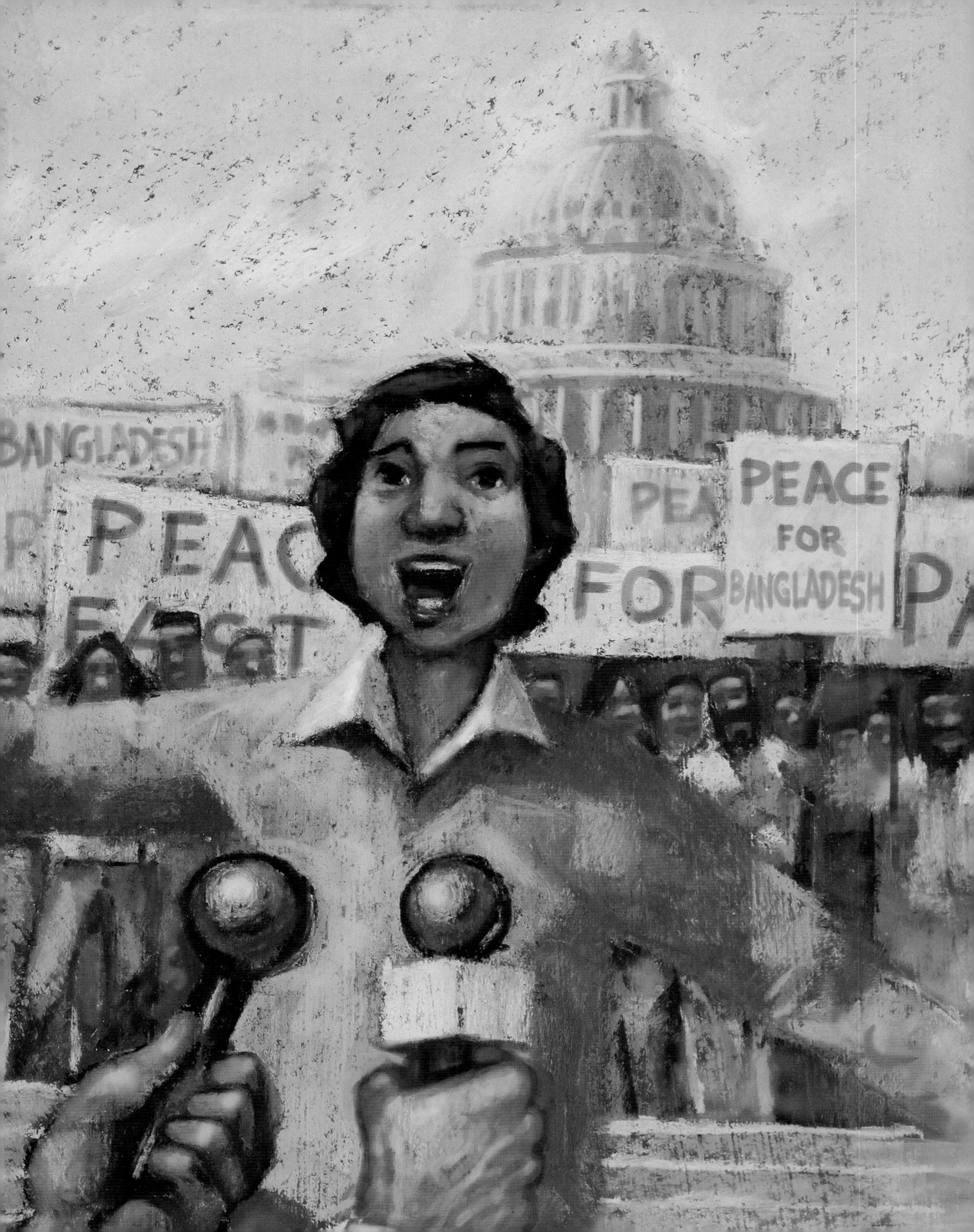
BANGLADESH
PEACE
FOR
BANGLADESH
FOR

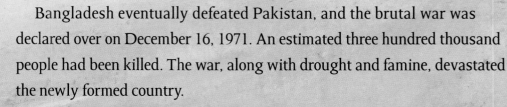

Bangladesh eventually defeated Pakistan, and the brutal war was declared over on December 16, 1971. An estimated three hundred thousand people had been killed. The war, along with drought and famine, devastated the newly formed country.

Muhammad realized it was time to return to Bangladesh. In 1972 he set out for home and accepted a job as head of the Economics Department at Chittagong University.

Now Muhammad saw firsthand how the war had affected his country. Every morning on his way to the university, he drove by the village of Jobra. The drought had destroyed the crops and left the villagers without food and fresh water. Barefoot children and their parents trudged along the dirt road toward the nearby fertile hills in desperate attempts to find food. Some returned clutching a few precious handfuls of rice and twigs to eat.

Muhammad was frustrated by all this poverty. Why was he teaching economics in a classroom when so many people in the village were suffering? Jobra became his new classroom. Over the next few years he interviewed many families so he could understand how they were surviving on very little.

In 1976 Muhammad met a young woman named Sufiya Begum. Her children slept in a mud hut while she wove bamboo into beautiful stools. She was weak and thin from lack of food, but the artistry of her work greatly impressed Muhammad.

Muhammad learned that Sufiya was one of many women who sold their crafts at the market to support their families. The bamboo used to make stools cost five *taka*, about twenty-two cents. Sufiya did not have twenty-two cents, so she had to borrow the money.

The banks in Jobra were not interested in loaning small amounts of money, and they did not want to risk making loans to poor people. So Sufiya had to go to a *mahajon*, a moneylender. The mahajon loaned her the twenty-two cents she needed, which she had to pay back with interest, a percentage of the amount she borrowed. But the mahajon took advantage of Sufiya and charged an unfairly high interest rate on her loan.

After Sufiya sold her stools and paid off her loan plus the interest, she was usually left with only two cents for herself. Two cents was not enough money to buy more bamboo. Two cents was not enough money to buy food for her family. As a result, Sufiya was forced to borrow more money from the mahajon.

Muhammad realized that Sufiya's life depended on just a few cents a day. He reached into his pocket. It jingled with many coins. He could easily give Sufiya the twenty-two cents she needed to buy more bamboo. Then she wouldn't owe the mahajon anything and could keep all the profits for herself.

But Muhammad hesitated. If he gave Sufiya the money, she would always be dependent on strangers for charity. Giving her the twenty-two cents would not solve her problems in the long run. He needed to figure out a way to help Sufiya and others in her situation break out of the cycle of poverty.

The next day Muhammad took a group of his students to Jobra. There they found forty-two women who needed a total of 856 taka—the equivalent of about twenty-seven dollars—to pay off their debts.

Muhammad then visited one of the largest banks in Bangladesh to ask for a loan with a fair interest rate for the women. The bank manager laughed at his request. Twenty-seven dollars was too small an amount for the bank to lend. And because the women were poor and did not know how to read and write, they were considered "banking untouchables." The bank did not trust them to pay back the loan.

The women had the same rights as everyone else, Muhammad believed. If the bank refused to help them, how could the women ever find a way to better their lives?

After being turned down by several banks, Muhammad decided to start a new bank that would lend money to the poor. In 1977 he launched Grameen Bank, which means "village bank" in the Bangla language of Bangladesh.

At Grameen Bank borrowers could take out loans of very small amounts of money with low interest rates. These small loans became known as microcredit.

Borrowers would be divided into groups of five, and each group would borrow an agreed upon amount. Then the group members would work together to pay back their loan on time. Muhammad believed that placing borrowers in groups would create a support system by which an entire group would be responsible for the success of each member.

At first it was difficult for Muhammad and his students to get women to sign up for his bank's loan program. The women did not understand how Muhammad's way of loaning money would be different from dealing with the mahajons.

Sometimes Muhammad and his students were also hindered by the rules of *purdah*, a practice that does not allow women to be seen interacting with men who are not their husbands. Often Muhammad could not approach a woman in public or in her home because it would be disrespectful. So he waited in the distance or outside a house while one of his female students talked to the women. On some days Muhammad waited patiently for hours in the pouring rain.

The patience and persistence of Muhammad and his students eventually paid off. They won the trust of the women, and many of them signed up for Grameen Bank's loan program.

At the bank the women learned to manage their finances. Each group took a seven-day training course to learn how banking worked. Muhammad also created a set of important lessons, the Sixteen Decisions, that the women had to memorize and follow. The lessons taught the women how to change their lives for the better by providing practical advice about positive habits such as drinking safely boiled water and making sure their children went to school.

To be approved for a loan, each group had to pass a test showing that the women understood the loan program. The women studied very hard and eventually everyone passed the test. Muhammad smiled as Sufiya clutched her group's loan of twenty-seven dollars as if it was a precious jewel.

Sufiya used her share of the loan to buy ingredients to cook sweets and materials to decorate bangles that she could sell alongside her bamboo stools at the market. She earned even more money than before, which was enough to pay back her portion of the loan and still provide for her family. She beamed with pride when she bought rice for her children with her hard-earned money.

Muhammad remembered the poor people who had stopped by his parents' house when he was a child. He remembered the homeless people and the slums he had seen when he was a Boy Scout and the starving people of Jobra he saw each day on his way to Chittagong University. And he remembered the day he met Sufiya Begum. Muhammad was grateful that he had found a way to help the poor create better lives for themselves.

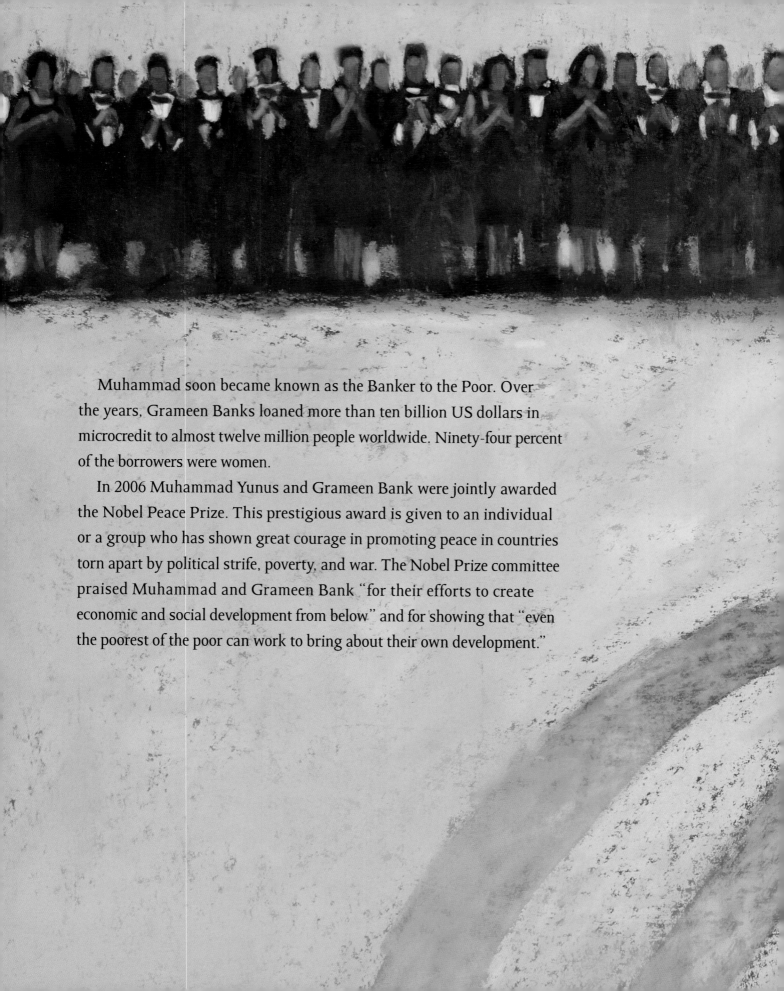

Muhammad soon became known as the Banker to the Poor. Over the years, Grameen Banks loaned more than ten billion US dollars in microcredit to almost twelve million people worldwide. Ninety-four percent of the borrowers were women.

In 2006 Muhammad Yunus and Grameen Bank were jointly awarded the Nobel Peace Prize. This prestigious award is given to an individual or a group who has shown great courage in promoting peace in countries torn apart by political strife, poverty, and war. The Nobel Prize committee praised Muhammad and Grameen Bank "for their efforts to create economic and social development from below" and for showing that "even the poorest of the poor can work to bring about their own development."

In his Nobel Peace Prize acceptance speech, Muhammad declared: "This year's prize gives highest honour and dignity to the hundreds of millions of women all around the world who struggle every day to make a living and bring hope for a better life for their children. This is a historic moment for them."

From helping one woman pay back her loan of twenty-two cents to providing billions of dollars in microcredit around the world, Muhammad Yunus has never stopped fighting for the poor. He still dreams of making the world a better place, a place where no woman, man, or child goes hungry. He still dreams of a world without poverty.

AFTERWORD

The success of Muhammad Yunus's Grameen Bank in Bangladesh has inspired many other countries, including Russia, Israel, Saudi Arabia, Mexico, Egypt, Ghana, China, and the Philippines, to start their own microfinance organizations. Ninety-seven percent of Grameen Bank customers around the world have successfully paid back their loans. Grameen Bank has also awarded more than 180,000 international scholarships to poor students so they can continue their education.

According to the 2012 US Census Bureau statistics, the average poverty threshold for a family of four in the United States is an annual income of $23,681. More than 46.5 million people in the United States live below the poverty line, including 16.1 million children. To live below the poverty line means that a person does not have an adequate supply of food.

In 2008 Grameen America opened in New York City. As of 2013, the bank had also opened branches in Charlotte, North Carolina; Indianapolis, Indiana; Omaha, Nebraska; and Los Angeles and the San Francisco area, California. Grameen America has given loans totaling approximately ninety-nine million dollars to more than forty-six thousand women. As a result, many low-income people have been able to become financially independent and lift themselves out of poverty.

In 2011 the government of Bangladesh forced Muhammad Yunus to resign from Grameen Bank, stating that at more than seventy years of age, he was beyond the legal age limit to hold the position of managing director. Professor Yunus and Grameen Bank filed an appeal for him to continue as head of the bank, but Bangladesh's Supreme Court rejected the appeal. So on May 12, 2011, Muhammad Yunus officially stepped down as managing director of Grameen Bank. He now chairs the Yunus Centre and is a cofounder of Grameen Creative Lab.

Courtesy of the Yunus Centre

Muhammad Yunus, age thirteen, as a Boy Scout

Both organizations have expanded beyond loaning money to the poor. They also embrace the concept of social business, promoting institutions whose primary purpose is to serve society and achieve a social goal in areas such as education, health care, nutrition, and green energy.

Today Muhammad Yunus lives in Bangladesh with his second wife, Afrozi Begum, a physics professor at Jahangirnagar University. His younger daughter, Deena, also lives in Bangladesh. His older daughter, Monica, from his first marriage to Vera Forostenko, is a professional opera singer who performs internationally with opera companies, including the Metropolitan Opera in New York, and other music groups.

In addition to the Nobel Peace Prize, Muhammad Yunus has received numerous other honors. Among

Nobel Laureate Muhammad Yunus with his Nobel Peace Prize medal and diploma, December 10, 2006

them are the World Food Prize (1994), which recognizes individuals who have helped improve the quality, quantity, or availability of food in the world; the Sydney Peace Prize (1998), awarded by Australia for work that achieves peace with justice; the United States Presidential Medal of Freedom (2009), given to individuals for significant contributions to cultural or public works; and the Congressional Gold Medal (2010), the highest civilian honor for achievement by an individual or institution awarded by the US Congress. Muhammad Yunus has also received forty-eight honorary doctorate degrees from universities the world over to honor his contributions to the field of economics and his efforts to eradicate global poverty.

Statistics about Grameen Bank were provided to the author by the Yunus Centre.

AUTHOR'S SOURCES

"Bangladesh and Pakistan: The Forgotten War." *TIME* Photos. http://content.time.com/time/photogallery/0,29307,1844754,00.html.

Bornstein, David. *The Price of a Dream: The Story of the Grameen Bank*. New York: Oxford University Press, 2005.

DeNavas-Walt, Carmen, Bernadette D. Proctor, and Jessica C. Smith. "Income, Poverty, and Health Insurance Coverage in the United States: 2012." Current Population Reports, United States Census Bureau. Washington, DC: US Government Printing Office, September 2013. http://www.census.gov/prod/2013pubs/p60-245.pdf.

Grameen America. http://grameenamerica.org/.

Grameen Bank: Bank for the Poor. http://www.grameen-info.org/index.php?option=com_frontpage&Itemid=68.

"Microcredit Pioneers Win Nobel Peace Prize." *USA Today*/Associated Press, October 13, 2006. http://www.usatoday.com/news/world/2006-10-13-norway-nobel_x.htm.

Nichols, Michelle. "'Banker to the Poor' Gives New York Women a Boost." Reuters, April 23, 2009. http://www.reuters.com/article/domesticNews/idUSTRE53M13G20090423?rpc=46.

"The Nobel Peace Prize 2006: Muhammad Yunus, Grameen Bank." Nobelprize.org, February 2014. http://www.nobelprize.org/nobel_prizes/peace/laureates/2006.

Reitz, Hans. "The Grameen Creative Lab—What is It?" PDF presentation given to the author, May 2009.

Siddiqi, Samana. "Statistics on Poverty and Food Wastage in America." SoundVision.com.http://www.soundvision.com/Info/poor/statistics.asp.

"What Are Poverty Thresholds and Poverty Guidelines?" Institute for Research on Poverty: University of Wisconsin-Madison. http://www.irp.wisc.edu/faqs/faq1.htm.

Wight, Vanessa R., Michelle Chau, and Yumiko Aratani. "Who Are America's Poor Children? The Official Story." NCCP: National Center for Children in Poverty, January 2010. http://www.nccp.org/publications/pub_912.html#1.

Yunus, Muhammad. "Nobel Lecture." Nobelprize.org. Oslo, Norway, December 10, 2006. http://www.nobelprize.org/nobel_prizes/peace/laureates/2006/yunus-lecture-en.html.

————. Personal interview with the author. Los Angeles, CA: Westin Hotel, May 24, 2009.

————, and Alan Jolis. *Banker to the Poor: Micro-Lending and the Battle Against World Poverty*. New York: Public Affairs, 1999.

QUOTATION SOURCES

Back cover: "I wanted . . . more ease." Muhammad Yunus, quoted in "Nobel Lecture." Nobelprize.org., December 10, 2006. http://www.nobelprize.org/nobel_prizes/peace/laureates/2006/yunus-lecture-en.html.

p. 9: "Learning from . . . greatest learning." Muhammad Yunus interview with the author. Westin Hotel, Los Angeles, CA, May 24, 2009.

p. 35: "for their efforts . . . development from below." Quoted in "The Nobel Peace Prize for 2006." Nobelprize.org., October 13, 2006. http://www.nobelprize.org/nobel_prizes/peace/laureates/2006/press.html.

"even the poorest . . . own development." Ibid.

p. 37: "This year's prize . . . moment for them." Muhammad Yunus, quoted in "Nobel Lecture." Nobelprize.org.